Awesome Asian Animals

Rhinoceroses

Are
Awesome!

by Allan Morey

Consultant: Jackie Gai, DVM
Wildlife Veterinarian
Vacaville, California

CAPSTONE PRESS
a capstone imprint

A+ Books are published by Capstone Press,
1710 Roe Crest Drive, North Mankato, Minnesota 56003
www.capstonepub.com

Library of Congress Cataloging-in-Publication Data
Morey, Allan, author.
Rhinoceroses are awesome! / by Allan Morey.
pages cm. — (A+ books. Awesome Asian animals)
Summary: "Introduces young readers to rhinoceroses, including physical characteristics, habitat, diet, behavior, and life cycle"— Provided by publisher.
Audience: Ages 4–8.
Audience: K to grade 3.
Includes bibliographical references and index.
ISBN 978-1-4914-3908-1 (library binding)
ISBN 978-1-4914-3927-2 (paperback)
ISBN 978-1-4914-3937-1 (eBook PDF)
1. Rhinoceroses—Juvenile literature. I. Title.
QL737.U63M67 2016
599.66'8—dc23   2014045607

Editorial Credits
Michelle Hasselius, editor; Peggie Carley, designer; Tracy Cummins, media researcher;
Morgan Walters, production specialist

Photo Credits
AP Photo: Achmad Ibrahim, 28, Kin Cheung, 27 Top; Capstone Press: 12; Dreamstime: Kmlauer, 19, Michael Elliott, Cover Bottom; FLPA: Alain Compost/Biosphoto, 13, Terry Whittaker, 15; Getty Images: Reto Puppetti, 5; iStockphoto: jezphotos, 27 Bottom, Matt Naylor, 18 Bottom; Minden Pictures: Suzi Eszterhas, 20, 21, ZSSD, 23, 26, 29 Left; Newscom: Suzi Eszterhas/Minden Pictures, 9; Shutterstock: Alan Jeffery, 22, Christian Musat, 17 Top, Eric Isselee, Cover Back, Cover Top, Cover Middle, 1, 6 Bottom, 30, 32 Bottom, Ewan Chesser, 6 Top, ilovezion, 7, JeremyRichards, 29 Right, Jonathan Tichon, 18 Top, kongsak sumano, 25, neelsky, 4, 16, 24, PeterVrabel, 8, Rigamondis, Design Element; Thinkstock: Anup Shah, 11; Wikimedia: Ltshears, 10, 14, 17 Bottom

Note to Parents, Teachers, and Librarians
This Awesome Asian Animals book uses full color photographs and a nonfiction format to introduce the concept of rhinoceroses. *Rhinoceroses Are Awesome!* is designed to be read aloud to a pre-reader or to be read independently by an early reader. Photographs help listeners and early readers understand the text and concepts discussed. The book encourages further learning by including the following sections: Table of Contents, Glossary, Read More, Internet Sites, Critical Thinking Using the Common Core, and Index. Early readers may need assistance using these features.

Printed in China.
042015   008864WMF15

Table of Contents

Amazing Rhinoceroses

Ba-boom! Ba-boom! The earth shakes. Heavy footsteps thud on the ground. A large animal bursts through the trees. Is it a tank with horns? No, it's a rhinoceros!

Rhinos are one of the world's largest land animals. But that is just one reason this animal is so amazing.

Tanks with Horns

An adult rhinoceros has a horn at the top of its nose. Rhinoceros actually means "nose horn." Some rhinos also have a small horn on their foreheads.

Rhino horns are similar to a horse's hooves or a turtle's beak. They are all made out of the same tough material, called keratin.

Rhinos look like they are wearing armor. But it's just thick folds of skin. The layers of skin keep rhinos from getting hurt as they stomp through forests.

Rhinos roll around in mud like pigs on a farm. Mud protects their skin from the hot sun and bug bites.

Rhinos are big. They can weigh up to 3 tons (2.7 metric tons), depending on the type of rhinoceros. That's as much as some cars weigh! Rhinos can stand more than 6 feet (1.8 meters) tall at the shoulders.

Rhinos cannot see well. But rhinos hear even the smallest sounds with their cup-shaped ears. Rhinos use their excellent sense of smell to find food.

Three of a Kind

Three types of rhinoceroses live in Asia. The Javan rhino is found only in Ujung Kulon National Park in Java, Indonesia. Less than 50 Javan rhinos live in the park. Javan rhinos are one of the rarest animals in the world.

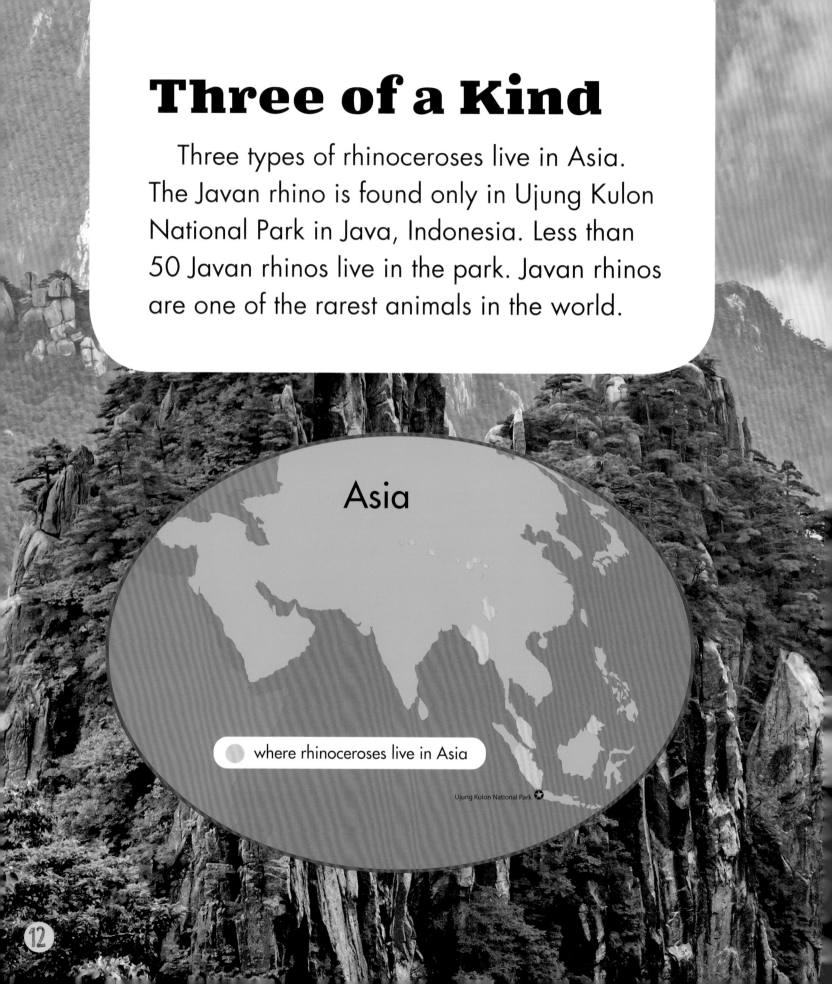

Asia

where rhinoceroses live in Asia

Ujung Kulon National Park ★

Javan rhino

The Sumatran rhino is sometimes called the hairy rhino. Unlike other rhinos, Sumatran rhinos are covered with dark hair.

Most Sumatran rhinos live in Indonesia. They roam through the country's forests and swamps. They can also be found in the mountain forests of Malaysia.

Indian rhinoceroses live mostly in northeastern India. Rivers often flood in this area. It's a good thing Indian rhinos can swim. They dive underwater in search of food. Indian rhinos also live in the forests and grasslands of southern Nepal. Sometimes Indian rhinoceroses are called greater one-horned rhinoceroses.

Chomp! Chomp! Rhinos are herbivores.
They eat plants that grow near their homes.
But rhinos aren't picky. They graze on
grasses. They eat fallen fruit and chew
on tree leaves. If they live near rivers,
they also eat plants that grow in the water.

Bulls, Cows, and Calves

Male rhinos are called bulls. Females are called cows. Bulls and cows spend most of their time apart. But they come together to mate.

A pregnant female gives birth to a calf after 15 to 16 months. Cows will have one calf every few years.

rhino calf

Calves can weigh more than 100 pounds
(45 kilograms) when they are born. Calves
stay with their mothers for two or three years.

Too Big to Eat

Adult rhinoceroses do not have predators in the wild. They are too big. Plus rhinos have deadly horns, sharp teeth, and tough skin. Most other animals leave them alone. But a hungry tiger might kill a young or sick rhino. A healthy rhino can live up to 40 years in the wild.

People are the biggest danger to
rhinoceroses. Rhinos once lived throughout
much of Africa and Asia. Now all three Asian
rhinos are in danger of becoming extinct.

People have killed thousands of rhinos for their horns. People use the horns to make medicines and jewelry.

Saving the Rhinos

Today wildlife groups raise money to help save rhinos. Governments made it against the law to hunt rhinos.

Together they have set up wildlife parks. Rhinos can safely live in these areas, and their numbers are growing.

Glossary

armor (AR-muhr)—a protective covering

extinct (ik-STINGKT)—no longer living; an extinct animal is one that has died out, with no more of its kind

graze (GRAYZ)—to eat grass and other plants

herbivore (HUR-buh-vor)—an animal that eats only plants

keratin (KAIR-uh-tin)—the hard substance that forms a rhinoceros' horns, a turtle's beak, and a horse's hooves

mate (MATE)—to join together to produce young

medicine (MED-uh-suhn)—a substance used to treat illnesses

predator (PRED-uh-tur)—an animal that hunts other animals for food

territory (TER-uh-tor-ee)—an area of land that an animal claims as its own to live in

Read More

Baxter, Bethany. *Indian Rhinoceroses.* Awesome Armored Animals. New York: PowerKids Press, 2014.

Ganeri, Anita. *Asia.* Introducing Continents. Chicago: Heinemann Library, 2014.

Snyder, Lydia. *Rhinos in Danger.* Animals at Risk. New York: Gareth Stevens Publishing, 2014.

Internet Sites

FactHound offers a safe, fun way to find Internet sites related to this book. All of the sites on FactHound have been researched by our staff.

Here's all you do:
Visit *www.facthound.com*
Type in this code: 9781491439081

 Check out projects, games and lots more at
www.capstonekids.com

Critical Thinking Using the Common Core

1. Turn to page 9. What is happening in this picture? Why do you think rhinos do this? (Integration of Knowledge and Ideas)

2. Rhinoceroses are herbivores. What is an herbivore? (Craft and Structure)

3. Rhinos have few predators in the wild. What are two reasons why? (Key Ideas and Details)

Index